French Short Stories for Beginners
Book 5

Over 100 Dialogues and Daily Used Phrases to Learn French in Your Car. Have Fun & Grow Your Vocabulary, with Crazy Effective Language Learning Lessons

LEARN LIKE A NATIVE

www.LearnLikeNatives.com

TABLE OF CONTENT

INTRODUCTION

Before we dive into some French, I want to congratulate you, whether you're just beginning, continuing, or resuming your language learning journey. Here at Learn Like a Native, we understand the determination it takes to pick up a new language and after reading this book, you'll be another step closer to achieving your language goals.

As a thank you for learning with us, we are giving you free access to our 'Speak Like a Native' eBook. It's packed full of practical advice and insider tips on how to make language learning quick, easy, and most importantly, enjoyable. Head over to LearnLikeNatives.com to access your free guide and peruse our huge selection of language learning resources.

Learning a new language is a bit like cooking—you need several different ingredients and the right technique, but the end result is sure to be delicious. We created this book of short stories for learning French because language is alive. Language is about the senses—hearing, tasting the words on your tongue, and touching another culture up close. Learning a language in a classroom is a fine place to start, but it's not a complete introduction to a language.

In this book, you'll find a language come to life. These short stories are miniature immersions into the French language, at a level that is perfect for beginners. This book is not a lecture on grammar. It's not an endless vocabulary list. This book is the closest you can come to a language immersion without leaving the country. In the stories within, you will see people speaking to each other, going through daily life situations, and using the most common, helpful words and phrases in language.

You are holding the key to bringing your French studies to life.

Made for Beginners

We made this book with beginners in mind. You'll find that the language is simple, but not boring. Most of the book is in the present tense, so you will be able to focus on dialogues, root verbs, and understand and find patterns in subject-verb agreement.

This is not "just" a translated book. While reading novels and short stories translated into French is a wonderful thing, beginners (and even novices) often run into difficulty. Literary licenses and complex sentence structure can make reading in your second language truly difficult—not to mention BORING. That's why French Short Stories for Beginners is the perfect book to pick up. The stories are simple, but not infantile. They were not written for children, but the language is simple so that beginners can pick it up.

The Benefits of Learning a Second Language

If you have picked up this book, it's likely that you are already aware of the many benefits of learning a second language. Besides just being fun, knowing more than one language opens up a whole new world to you. You will be able to communicate with a much larger chunk of the world. Opportunities in the workforce will open up, and maybe even your day-to-day work will be improved. Improved communication can also help you expand your business. And from a neurological perspective, learning a second language is like taking your daily vitamins and eating well, for your brain!

How To Use The Book

The chapters of this book all follow the same structure:

- A short story with several dialogs
- A summary in French
- A list of important words and phrases and their English translation
- Questions to test your understanding
- Answers to check if you were right
- The English translation of the story to clear every doubt

You may use this book however is comfortable for you, but we have a few recommendations for getting the most out of the experience. Try these tips and if they work for you, you can use them on every chapter throughout the book.

1) Start by reading the story all the way through. Don't stop or get hung up on any particular words or phrases. See how much of the plot you can understand in this way. We think you'll get a lot more of it than you may expect, but it is completely normal not to understand everything in the story. You are learning a new language, and that takes time.

2) Read the summary in French. See if it matches what you have understood of the plot.

3) Read the story through again, slower this time. See if you can pick up the meaning of any words or phrases you don't understand by using context clues and the information from the summary.

4) Test yourself! Try to answer the five comprehension questions that come at the end of each story. Write your answers

down, and then check them against the answer key. How did you do? If you didn't get them all, no worries!

5) Look over the vocabulary list that accompanies the chapter. Are any of these the words you did not understand? Did you already know the meaning of some of them from your reading?

6) Now go through the story once more. Pay attention this time to the words and phrases you haven't understand. If you'd like, take the time to look them up to expand your meaning of the story. Every time you read over the story, you'll understand more and more.

7) Move on to the next chapter when you are ready.

_*www.LearnLikeNatives.com*

Read and Listen

The audio version is the best way to experience this book, as you will hear a native French speaker tell you each story. You will become accustomed to their accent as you listen along, a huge plus for when you want to apply your new language skills in the real world.

If this has ignited your language learning passion and you are keen to find out what other resources are available, go to LearnLikeNatives.com, where you can access our vast range of free learning materials. Don't know where to begin? An excellent place to start is our 'Speak Like a Native' free eBook, full of practical advice and insider tips on how to make language learning quick, easy, and most importantly, enjoyable.

12

And remember, small steps add up to great advancements! No moment is better to begin learning than the present.

www.LearnLikeNatives.com

FREE BOOK!

Get the *FREE BOOK* that reveals the
secrets path to learn any language fast,
and without leaving your country.

Discover:

- The **language 5 golden rules** to
  master languages at will

- Proven **mind training techniques** to
  revolutionize your learning

- A complete step-by-step guide to
  conquering any language

CHAPTER 1
New Roommates /
Common everyday objects +
possession

HISTOIRE

Aujourd'hui, c'est le jour de l'emménagement à l'université. Les étudiants de première année amènent **leurs** affaires dans le dortoir.

Anna arrive à l'université avec ses parents. **Sa** voiture est pleine de **cartons**. Anna apporte avec elle tout ce dont elle a besoin pour une année scolaire. Ils se garent à l'extérieur du dortoir d'Anna. Le bâtiment est un grand bâtiment en briques. Il semble ennuyeux. Anna essaie de rester positive. « Cette année sera formidable », se dit-elle.

Sa famille commence à décharger la voiture. Anna est complètement prête. Ils déchargent des cartons pleins de ses affaires. Son frère l'aide à monter les boîtes dans sa chambre. La chambre est petite. Il y a deux lits. Anna aura une colocataire.

Le premier carton qu'Anna ouvre contient des fournitures scolaires. Elle met ses **blocs-notes**, ses **crayons** et ses **stylos** sur son bureau. La chambre n'est pas décorée, il n'y a qu'une **télévision** sur le mur. Anna range ses affaires dans la chambre. Elle prend son **calendrier** pour le mettre au mur.

« Ce n'est pas **le mien**! » dit-elle. « C'est un calendrier de jolies femmes. C'est **le sien** », dit Anna en pointant son frère du doigt.

« Oh, désolé », dit son frère. Anna le jette à la **poubelle**. La famille rit.

On frappe à la porte. Ils ouvrent la porte. Une fille blonde se tient dehors. Elle est avec une femme plus âgée, sa mère.

« Bonjour, je suis Beatriz », dit la fille.

« Je suis Anna, dit Anna. Je suppose que nous sommes colocataires! »

« D'où venez-vous ? » demande Beatriz.

« Pas loin, à seulement une heure au nord », explique Anna.

« Moi aussi ! » dit Beatriz.

Les filles se serrent la main et sourient. Beatriz porte ses propres cartons. Les familles aident leurs filles à défaire leurs affaires.

Les premiers jours à l'université sont agréables. Anna se fait de nouveaux amis. Beatriz et elle s'entendent très bien. Anna va assiste à ses nouvelles classes. Tout est parfait. Cependant, quelque chose ne va pas. Certaines des affaires d'Anna commencent à disparaître. D'abord, elle ne trouve pas sa **brosse.** Puis, le lendemain, elle se regarde dans le cabinet du **miroir**. Elle voit sa **lotion** mais son **parfum** a disparu. Quand elle rentre de ses cours ce soir-là, elle met de la musique. Il n'y a pas de son. Son **haut-parleur** n'est plus là!

Elle demande à Beatriz. « Beatriz », dit-elle. « Est-ce qu'il te manque quelque chose? »

« Oui! » dit Beatriz. « Mon **ordinateur portable**. Je panique. »

« Oh non! » dit Anna. « Il me manque aussi des choses. »

Il manque maintenant trois choses à Anna. Elle appelle sa mère sur son **téléphone portable**.

« Bonjour, maman », dit Anna.

« Salut, chérie, dit sa mère. Comment va l'école? »

« Très bien, dit Anna. Mais mes affaires continuent à disparaître. »

« Que veux-tu dire? » demande sa mère. Anna parle à sa mère du parfum disparu, du haut-parleur disparu et de la brosse disparue.

« C'est tellement étrange, dit sa mère. Les as-tu emmenés quelque part? »

« Non, maman, dit Anna. Je n'ai jamais quitté la chambre. Le reste du **système stéréo** est ici. Mon **lecteur mp3** aussi. »

« Verrouilles-tu ta porte? » demande sa mère.

« Oui, maman ! » dit Anna. « Et c'est juste le parfum qui est parti. J'ai encore tout le reste du **maquillage, du rouge à lèvres**, tout ! »

« Penses-tu que ce pourrait être Beatriz? » demande sa mère.

« Non, il lui manque aussi des choses », dit Anna.

« Ok, va vérifier avec le bureau des objets trouvés », dit la mère d'Anna.

« Ok! Je dois y aller », dit Anna.

Anna raccroche. L'idée de sa mère est bonne. Elle descend au bureau du dortoir. Elle demande à voir la boîte des objets perdus. La boite est pleine. Elle regarde à l'intérieur. Elle trouve des **cahiers**, une **caméra** et même un **peigne**. Mais elle ne voit pas ses affaires. Elle regarde mieux. Elle voit un **ordinateur** portable.

« Est-ce **le tien**? » demande-t-elle en pensant à Beatriz. Elle l'enlève. Il l'est. Elle prend l'ordinateur pour le donner à Beatriz. Au moins, elle trouve quelque chose.

Elle monte. Elle donne l'ordinateur à Beatriz.

« Oh, Anna, c'est **mon** ordinateur! » dit Beatriz. « Merci beaucoup. »

« De rien », dit Anna. « Je suis tellement heureuse d'avoir trouvé **ton** ordinateur. »

« Moi aussi, dit Beatriz. As-tu trouvé **tes** affaires? »

« Non », dit Anna.

« Dommage », dit Beatriz. Les filles s'endorment.

Le lendemain, Beatriz a cours. Anna reste dans la chambre. Elle travaille sur un projet, et utilise des **ciseaux** pour couper des photos à coller sur un **dossier**. Elle pense à ses objets disparus. Peut-être qu'elle devrait regarder dans la chambre. Elle regarde partout. Puis elle se tourne vers le placard de Beatriz. Elle l'ouvre. Elle regarde à l'intérieur.

« C'est à moi! » dit Anna. Elle sort sa brosse. Elle est stupéfaite. Pourquoi sa brosse est-elle dans le placard de Beatriz? Elle regarde de plus près. Sous une pile de **vêtements**, elle sent quelque chose de dur. Elle le prend. C'est son flacon de parfum! Quand elle regarde mieux, elle trouve son haut-parleur, aussi.

« C'était Beatriz tout le temps », dit Anna. Le **téléphone** de la chambre sonne. Anna répond. C'est la mère de Beatriz.

« Bonjour, Anna, dit la mère de Beatriz. Comment allez-vous? »

« Très bien, dit Anna. Beatriz n'est pas là. »

« Pouvez-vous lui dire que j'ai appelé? » demande la mère de Beatriz.

« Oui, mais, puis-je vous parler de quelque chose? » demande Anna.

« Bien sûr », dit la mère de Beatriz.

« Certaines de mes affaires ont disparu, dit Anna. Et j'en ai trouvé beaucoup dans le placard de **votre** fille. »

« Oh, non, dit la mère de Beatriz. Je dois vous dire quelque chose. »

« Quoi? » dit Anna.

« Beatriz est kleptomane », dit sa mère. « Elle prend des choses et les rend exactement sept jours plus tard. Elle vous les rendra d'ici demain. »

« Que dois-je faire? » demande Anna.

« Il suffit d'attendre qu'elle les rende », dit sa mère.

« D'accord », dit Anna.

« Merci de votre compréhension », dit la mère de Beatriz.

RÉSUMÉ

Anna et Beatriz sont colocataires. C'est leur première année à l'université. Elles se rencontrent le jour de leur emménagement. Elles rangent leur chambre. Leurs parents les aident. Elles s'entendent bien. Au cours de la première semaine, beaucoup d'affaires d'Anna disparaissent. Elle ne les trouve nulle part. Des objets de Beatriz disparaissent aussi. Anna regarde partout. Elle regarde dans les objets trouvés, où elle trouve l'ordinateur disparu de Beatriz. Quand Beatriz n'est pas là, Anna regarde dans son placard. Elle trouve toutes ses affaires. La mère de Beatriz appelle. Elle dit à Anna que Beatriz est kleptomane.

Liste de vocabulaire

their	leur
her	son
boxes	boîtes
mine	mien
notepads	blocs-notes
pencils	crayons
pens	stylos
television	télévision
calendar	calendrier
his	son
trash can	poubelle
brush	brosse
mirror	miroir
lotion	lotion
perfume	parfum

speaker	haut-parleur
computer	ordinateur
cell phone	téléphone portable
stereo system	système stéréo
makeup	maquillage
lipstick	rouge à lèvres
notebook	Carnet
video camera	caméra vidéo
comb	peigne
my	mon
yours	votre
your	votre
scissors	ciseaux
clothes	vêtements
telephone	téléphone
your	votre

QUESTIONS

1) Comment Beatriz et Anna se connaissent-elles?

    a) elles ont toujours été amies

    b) elles se rencontrent en classe

    c) elles sont colocataires

    d) elles fréquentent la même école

2) Lequel de ces éléments n'a pas disparu?

    a) la brosse

    b) le parfum

    c) le haut-parleur

    d) le miroir

3) Que suggère la mère d'Anna?

    a) qu'Anna rentre à la maison

    b) qu'Anna confronte Beatriz

c) qu'Anna achète une nouvelle brosse

d) qu'Anna cherche dans les objets trouvés

4) Que trouve Anna dans les objets trouvés?

a) son pinceau

b) l'ordinateur de Beatriz

c) un sweat-shirt

d) son parfum

5) Qu'est-il arrivé aux affaires d'Anna?

a) Beatriz les a prises et les a mises dans son placard

b) Anna les a perdues

c) Anna les a jetées

d) rien

RÉPONSES

1) Comment Beatriz et Anna se connaissent-elles?

c) elles sont colocataires

2) Lequel de ces éléments n'a pas disparu?

d) le miroir

3) Que suggère la mère d'Anna?

d) qu'Anna cherche dans les objets trouvés

4) Que trouve Anna dans les objets trouvés?

b) l'ordinateur de Beatriz

5) Qu'est-il arrivé aux affaires d'Anna?

a) Beatriz les a prises et les a mises dans son placard

Translation of the Story

New Roommates

STORY

Today is move-in day at the university. First year students move **their** things into the dormitory.

Anna arrives to the university with her parents. **Her** car is loaded with **boxes**. Anna brings everything she needs for a year of school with her. They park outside of Anna's dormitory. The building is a big, brick building. It looks boring. Anna tries to think positive. This year will be great, she tells herself.

Her family begins to unload the car. Anna is very prepared. They take out boxes full of her things. Her brother helps her take the boxes up to the room. The room is small. There are two beds. Anna will have a roommate.

The first box Anna opens has school supplies. She puts her **notepads**, **pencils** and **pens** on her desk. The room has no decoration, except for a **television** on the wall. Anna organizes her things in the room. She takes her **calendar** out to put on the wall.

"This isn't **mine**!" she says. It is a calendar of pretty women.

"This is **his**," Anna says, pointing at her brother.

"Oh, sorry," says her brother. Anna throws it in the **trash can**. The family laughs.

There is a knock on the door. They open the door. A blonde girl stands outside. She is with an older woman, her mother.

"Hello, I'm Beatriz," says the girl.

"I'm Anna," says Anna. "I guess we are roommates!"

"Where are you from?" asks Beatriz.

"Nearby, just an hour north," says Anna.

"Me too!" says Beatriz.

The girls shake hands and smile. Beatriz brings her own boxes. The families help their daughters unpack.

The first days of school are nice. Anna makes new friends. She and Beatriz get along great. Anna goes to her new classes. Everything is perfect. However, one thing is wrong. Some of Anna's belongings begin to disappear. First, she can't find her **brush**. Then, the next day, she looks in the **mirror**. She sees her **lotion** but her **perfume** is missing. When she arrives from class that evening, she puts on some music. There is no sound. Her **speaker** is gone!

She asks Beatriz. "Beatriz," she says. "Are you missing anything?"

"Yes!" says Beatriz. "My laptop **computer**. I am freaking out."

"Oh no!" says Anna. "I am missing a few things, too."

Anna is missing three things now. She calls her mother on her **cell phone**.

"Hi, mom," says Anna.

"Hi, honey," says her mom. "How is school?"

"Fine," says Anna. "But my belongings keep disappearing."

"What do you mean?" asks her mom. Anna tells her mom about the missing perfume, the missing speaker, and the missing brush.

"That is so strange," says her mom. "Did you take them somewhere?"

"No, mom," says Anna. "I never left the room. The rest of the **stereo system** is here. My **mp3 player,** too."

"Do you lock your door?" asks her mom.

"Yes, mom!" says Anna. "And it's just the perfume that is gone. I still have all the other **makeup**, **lipstick**, everything!"

"Do you think it could be Beatriz?" asks her mom.

"No way, she is missing stuff too," says Anna.

"Ok, go check the lost-and-found," says Anna's mom.

"Ok! Gotta go," says Anna.

Anna hangs up the phone. Her mom's idea is good. She goes downstairs to the dormitory office. She asks to see the lost-and-found box. The box is full. She looks through it. She finds **notebooks**, a **video camera**, and even a **comb**. But does not see her things. She looks more. She sees a laptop **computer**.

"Is that **yours**?" she asks, thinking of Beatriz. She pulls it out. It is. She takes the computer to give to Beatriz. At least she finds something.

She goes upstairs. She gives Beatriz the computer.

"Wow, Anna, it's **my** computer!" says Beatriz. "Thank you so much."

"You're welcome," says Anna. "So glad I found **your** computer."

"Me too," says Beatriz. "Did you find any of your things?"

"No," says Anna.

"Bummer," says Beatriz. The girls go to sleep.

The next day, Beatriz has class. Anna stays in the dorm room. She works on a project, using **scissors** to cut pictures to glue on a **folder**. She thinks about her missing items. Maybe she should look in the dorm room. She looks everywhere. Then she turns to Beatriz's closet. She opens it. She looks inside it.

"This is mine!" says Anna. She pulls out her brush. She is shocked. Why is her brush in Beatriz's closet? She looks closer. Under a stack of **clothes**, she feels something hard. She pulls it out. It is her bottle of perfume! When she looks closer, she finds her speaker, too.

"It was Beatriz the whole time," says Anna. The room **telephone** rings. Anna answers. It is Beatriz's mom.

"Hi, Anna," says Beatriz's mom. "How are you?"

"Fine," says Anna. "Beatriz isn't here."

"Can you tell her I called?" asks Beatriz's mom.

"Yes, but, can I talk to you about something?" asks Anna.

"Sure," says Beatriz's mom.

"Some of my things have gone missing," says Anna. "And I just found many of them in **your** daughter's closet."

"Oh, no," says Beatriz's mom. "I need to tell you something."

"What?" says Anna.

"Beatriz is a kleptomaniac," says her mom. "She takes things and then returns them exactly seven days later. She will return those items to you by tomorrow."

"What do I do?" asks Anna.

"Just wait for her to return them," says her mom.

"Okay," says Anna.

"Thank you for understanding," says Beatriz's mom.

CHAPTER 2
A Day in the Life / transition words

HISTOIRE

Bey se réveille dans une chambre d'hôtel. Elle est fatiguée. Son corps est fatigué, **mais** son esprit est encore plus fatigué. Elle se sent seule. Ses amis et sa famille ne comprennent pas ce que c'est d'être célèbre. Elle rit. Ils veulent être célèbres. Ils veulent passer une journée de sa vie. Les gens pensent que les célébrités s'amusent toute la journée. Ils pensent que les célébrités obtiennent tout ce qu'elles veulent. **Cependant**, Bey sait que ce n'est pas vrai.

Pourquoi les gens veulent-ils être célèbres? Bey pense. Elle se fait un café. Les médias la présentent comme un succès. Les gens recherchent le succès. Ils veulent une vie parfaite. **Par conséquent**, ils essaient de devenir célèbres. Elle sait que la vie n'est pas parfaite.

L'horloge indique sept heures. Sa journée est remplie. **Donc**, elle doit se lever tôt. Certaines personnes pensent que les célébrités dorment jusqu'à tard. Elle a beaucoup à faire. Il n'y a pas le temps de dormir tard. Elle entend la sonnette.

« Bonjour, » dit Bey.

« Bonjour, Bey », disent les trois femmes. Une femme est sa styliste. Une autre femme est sa maquilleuse. **Enfin**, la coiffeuse entre. Elle ouvre la porte. Elles rentrent. Elles commencent à travailler.

« Quelle chemise ? » dit le styliste.

« Quelle couleur de rouge à lèvres ? » demande le maquilleur.

« Pourquoi as-tu dormi avec tes cheveux comme ça ? » demande le coiffeur.

Le café de Bey est froid. Elle fait un autre café. **Ensuite**, elle répond à toutes les questions. Elles l'aident. **Enfin**, elle est prête.

Elle quitte l'hôtel à 10 heures. Il y a beaucoup de gens à l'extérieur. Ils l'attendent. Quand elle sort, ils crient. Ils prennent des photos. Bey monte dans une voiture. La voiture a des fenêtres teintées. Personne ne peut voir à l'intérieur. **Par conséquent**, elle peut faire ce qu'elle veut. Elle se détend. Son téléphone sonne.

« Bonjour ? » dit-elle.

« Bey, où es-tu ? » demande son manager.

« Dans la voiture », dit-elle.

« Tu es en retard! » dit le directeur.

« Désolé, » dit Bey. Elle a un cours de danse, des cours de voix et une séance photos. Une journée bien remplie. Son agent tient son emploi du temps. Il lui dit quoi faire. Il lui dit quand y aller. Elle se sent coincée. Elle doit travailler pour rester célèbre. Elle ne peut pas prendre de vacances.

La voiture s'arrête. **D'abord**, Bey fait une séance photo. C'est pour un magazine. Une fille maquille sur Bey. C'est une fan. Elle sourit.

« Comment allez-vous ? » demande-t-elle.

« Très bien », dit Bey.

« Je suis votre fan », dit-elle.

« Merci », dit Bey.

« Je chante aussi », dit la jeune fille. Elle poudre le visage de Bey.

« Vraiment ? » demande Bey. Elle s'ennuie.

« Oui. Je veux être célèbre! » dit la fille.

« Être célèbre, c'est beaucoup de travail! » dit Bey.

« Je m'en fous! » dit la fille.

« Que faites-vous ce soir ? », demande Bey.

« Un dîner avec mon petit ami, une promenade dans le parc, peut-être visiter un musée », dit la jeune fille.

« J'ai du travail, un concert, dit Bey. **En fait**, j'en ai un tous les soirs. Je ne peux pas aller au parc **parce que** les gens me reconnaissent. Ils ne me laissent pas tranquille. »

« Oh », dit la fille. Elle finit le maquillage.

« **Par exemple**, je n'arrive pas à me souvenir d'une visite dans un musée », dit Bey. Elle a fini. On prend des photos d'elle. Sa robe est glamour.

Elle est belle et heureuse. Elle dit au revoir et monte dans la voiture.

Ensuite, Bey a un cours de danse. Son cours est dans un studio de danse. Son professeur est un professionnel. Ils s'entraînent pour le concert. Le concert de ce soir est dans un stade de New York. Elle oublie la danse de sa chanson la plus célèbre. Elle s'entraîne pendant deux heures. **Sans le moindre doute**, elle connaît la danse.

Après, Bey a des cours de voix. Les chanteurs célèbres ont besoin de cours. Les cours de voix les aident à chanter facilement. C'est important. **Après tout**, c'est difficile de chanter à un concert tous les soirs.

Après le cours de voix, elle prend son déjeuner. Son assistante le lui apporte. Même si c'est rapide, c'est sain. Elle a un smoothie et une salade. Peu après, elle doit se préparer pour le concert.

Elle vérifie son téléphone. Bey a une autre assistante. Cette assistante s'occupe des réseaux sociaux. Elle met des photos sur Instagram et sur Facebook. **En fin de compte**, Bey aime vérifier elle-même. Sa nouvelle photo a 1 000 000 « j'aime ». Pas mal, pense-t-elle. Elle a aussi beaucoup de commentaires. Certains sont méchants, **alors** Bey éteint son téléphone. Elle essaie d'être positive.

Dans la voiture, Bey appelle ses amis. Elle parle à sa mère. Elle parle dans la voiture **puisqu'**elle n'a pas beaucoup de temps. Elle est fatiguée. Elle a mal à la tête. Elle peut peut-être faire la sieste. Elle regarde son téléphone. Il est trop tard pour faire la sieste.

Pendant que Bey se prépare, les fans attendent. Ils font la queue dehors. Ils sont excités. Ils ont payé beaucoup d'argent pour les billets.

Maintenant, elle a mal à la gorge. Elle boit du thé chaud. Si elle ne peut pas chanter, les fans seront tristes. Elle regarde son téléphone. Elle a une photo sauvegardée pour ces moments-là. Il s'agit d'une lettre.

« Cher Bey », dit-il.

« Tu es ma chanteuse préférée. Je pense que tu es incroyable. Je veux être comme toi quand je serai grande. Je t'aime, Susy. » C'est une fan de 7 ans. Bey se souvient d'elle. Elle sourit. Il y a des centaines de filles comme Susy au concert. Pour cette raison, elle chante sur scène.

Finalement, le concert se termine.

De plus en plus de fans demandent l'autographe de Bey. Ils sourient. Ils prennent des photos sur leur téléphone. Elle imagine leur vie. Ils vont à des fêtes. Ils voient des amis. Ils vont au restaurant. **Dans tous les cas**, ils sont libres. Elle est jalouse. **Même s**'ils ne sont pas célèbres, ils ont une meilleure vie.

Elle pense à la maquilleuse d'aujourd'hui. Elle se demande, que fait-elle maintenant ? Bey pense qu'elle va peut-être arrêter.

Tout à coup, son téléphone fait un bruit.

C'est un rappel pour aller se coucher. Demain est une autre journée chargée.

RÉSUMÉ

Bey est une célébrité. C'est une chanteuse de pop célèbre. Les gens sont jaloux de sa vie. Cependant, ce n'est pas facile. Sa journée commence tôt. Ses trois assistantes viennent à l'hôtel. Elles la préparent. Ensuite, elle a une journée bien remplie. Elle va à une séance photo. La maquilleuse veut être célèbre. Bey dit que ce n'est pas génial. Bey pratique la danse et le chant. Puis elle se prépare pour son concert. Elle se sent malade. Cependant, elle se produit pour ses nombreux fans. Elle prend des photos et signe des autographes. Elle est jalouse de la vie normale de ses fans.

Liste de vocabulaire

but	mais
however	toutefois
as a result	en conséquence

therefore	par conséquent
lastly	enfin
then	alors
finally	enfin
therefore	par conséquent
first	premièrement
in fact	en fait
because	parce que
for example	par exemple
second	deuxième
without a doubt	sans aucun doute
after all	après tout
even though	même si
ultimately	en fin de compte
so	donc
since	depuis

while	tandis que
if	si
for this reason	pour cette raison
eventually.	finalement.
either way	de toute façon
despite	malgré
all of a sudden	tout d'un coup

QUESTIONS

1) Quelle personne ne vient pas à l'hôtel de Bey ?

    a) une maquilleuse

    b) une styliste

    c) une fan

    d) une coiffeuse

2) Pourquoi le directeur de Bey l'appelle-t-il?

a) pour demander où elle est

b) pour la renvoyer

c) pour la féliciter

d) pour demander comment elle va

3) Quel est le travail de Bey ?

a) danseuse

b) pop star

c) animatrice d'une émission-débat

d) photographe

4) Que fait Bey pour l'aider à chanter ?

a) elle boit du thé

b) elle va à des cours de voix

c) elle prie

d) elle croise les doigts

5) Que signale la notification du téléphone à la fin de l'histoire?

a) quelqu'un appelle

b) il est temps de prendre des médicaments

c) une notification d'Instagram

d) il est temps de se coucher

RÉPONSES

1) Quelle personne ne vient pas à l'hôtel de Bey ?

c) une fan

2) Pourquoi le directeur de Bey l'appelle-t-il?

a) pour demander où elle est

3) Quel est le travail de Bey ?

b) pop star

4) Que fait Bey pour l'aider à chanter ?

b) elle va à des cours de voix

5) Que signale la notification du téléphone à la fin de l'histoire?

d) il est temps de se coucher

Translation of the Story

A Day in the Life

STORY

Bey wakes up in a hotel room. She is tired. Her body is tired, **but** her mind is more tired. She feels alone. Her friends and family don't understand what it is like to be famous. She laughs. They want to be famous. They want to spend a day in her life. People think celebrities have fun all day. They think celebrities get anything they want. **However,** Bey knows this is not true.

Why do people want to be famous? Bey thinks. She makes a coffee. The media shows her as success. People want success. They want a perfect life. **As a result,** they try to become famous. She knows life is not perfect.

The clock says seven o'clock. Her day is busy. **Therefore**, she has to wake up early. Some people think celebrities sleep late. She has a lot to do. There is no time to sleep late. She hears the doorbell.

"Hello," says Bey.

"Hi, Bey," say the three women. One woman is her stylist. Another woman is her makeup artist. **Lastly**, the hairdresser enters. She opens the door. They go inside. They begin to work.

"Which shirt?" says the stylist.

"Which color of lipstick?" asks the makeup artist.

"Why did you sleep with your hair like that?" asks the hairdresser.

Bey's coffee is cold. She makes another coffee. **Then**, she answers all the questions. They help her. **Finally,** she is ready.

She leaves the hotel at 10 a.m. There are many people outside. They wait for her. When she goes out, they scream. They take pictures. Bey gets in a car. The car has dark windows. No one can see in. **Therefore,** she can do what she wants. She relaxes. Her phone rings.

"Hello?" she says.

"Bey, where are you?" asks her manager.

"In the car," she says.

"You're late!" says the manager.

"Sorry," said Bey. She has dance practice, voice lessons, and a photo shoot. A busy day. Her manager keeps her schedule. He tells her what to do. He tells her when to go. She feels stuck. She must work to stay famous. She can't take a vacation.

The car stops. **First**, Bey has a photo shoot. It is for a magazine. A girl puts makeup on Bey. She is a fan. She smiles.

"How are you?" she asks.

"Fine," says Bey.

"I am your fan," she says.

"Thank you," says Bey.

"I sing, too," the girl says. She powders Bey's face.

"Really?" asks Bey. She is bored.

"Yes. I want to be famous!" says the girl.

"Being famous is a lot of work!" says Bey.

"I don't care!" says the girl.

"What are you doing tonight?" asks Bey.

"Dinner with my boyfriend, a walk in the park, maybe visit a museum," says the girl.

"I have work, a concert," says Bey. "**In fact,** I have one every night. I can't go out to the park **because** people recognize me. They don't leave me alone."

"Oh," says the girl. She finishes the makeup.

"**For example**, I can't remember a visit to a museum," says Bey. She is finished. She takes her pictures. Her dress is glamorous. She looks beautiful and happy. She says goodbye and gets in the car.

Second, Bey has dance practice. She practices in a dance studio. Her teacher is professional. They practice for the concert. Tonight's concert is in a stadium in New York City. She forgets the dance for her most famous song. She practices for two hours. **Without a doubt**, she knows the dance.

Third, Bey has voice lessons. Famous singers need lessons. Voice lessons help them sing easily. This is important. **After all,** singing a concert every night is difficult.

After voice, she eats lunch. Her assistant brings it to her. Even though it is quick, it is healthy. She has a smoothie and a salad. Soon she must prepare for the concert.

She checks her phone. Bey has another assistant. This assistant does social media. She puts pictures on Instagram and Facebook. **Ultimately**, Bey likes to see for herself. Her new picture has 1,000,000 likes. Not bad, she thinks. It also has many comments. Some are mean, **so** Bey turns off her phone. She tries to be positive.

In the car, Bey calls her friends. She talks to her mother. She talks in the car **since** she doesn't have much time. She is tired. She has a headache. Maybe she can nap. She looks at her phone. It is too late to nap.

While Bey gets ready, fans wait. They make a line outside. They are excited. They paid a lot of money for the tickets.

Now her throat hurts. She drinks warm tea. **If** she can't sing, the fans will be sad. She looks at her phone. She has a picture saved for these moments. It is a letter.

"Dear Bey," it says.

"You are my favorite singer. I think you are amazing. I want to be just like you when I grow up. Love, Susy." It is from a 7-year-old fan. Bey remembers her. She smiles. There are hundreds of girls like Susy at the concert. **For this reason,** she performs.

Eventually, the concert ends.

More and more fans ask for Bey's autograph. They smile. They take pictures on their phone. She imagines their lives. They go to parties. They see friends. They go to restaurants. **Either way**, they have freedom. She is jealous. **Despite** not being famous, they have better lives.

She thinks of the makeup girl from today. She wonders, what is she doing now? Bey thinks maybe she will quit.

All of a sudden, her phone makes a sound.

It is a reminder to go to bed. Tomorrow is another busy day.

CHAPTER 3

The Camino Inspiration / Numbers + Family

Molly adore les aventures.

Elle est la personne la plus courageuse de sa **famille**, encore plus courageuse que ses **deux frères**. Elle va souvent camper avec sa famille dans les bois. Ce week-end, ils vont ensemble à la montagne. La lune brille et les oiseaux et les animaux sont silencieux. Molly s'assoit avec ses frères et sa sœur près du feu, ils parlent et ils jouent. Ils voient une chauve-souris voler au-dessus de leur tête.

« Ewww! » crie la sœur de Molly.

« Une chauve-souris! » crie **un** des frères de Molly.

Puis, **trois** autres chauves-souris volent au-dessus de leur tête.

« Ahhh! Allons chercher **maman** et **papa**! » s'écrie l'autre frère, John.

« Ce n'est qu'une chauve-souris », dit Molly.

D'autres chauves-souris arrivent, jusqu'à ce qu'il y en ait **huit** qui volent au-dessus d'eux. La sœur et les frères de Molly disparaissent dans leurs tentes, effrayés. Molly ne bouge pas. Elle regarde les chauves-souris voler en rond, maintenant il y en a **dix-neuf**, non, **vingt**!

« Salut, Molly », dit sa **mère**, qui marche derrière son **père** en direction du feu de camp.

« Oh, il y a assurément beaucoup de chauves-souris dans ces bois, dit son père. N'as-tu pas peur? »

Molly secoue la tête non, et regarde les chauves-souris s'envoler dans le ciel étoilé.

« Dînons! » dit-elle. Ses frères et sa sœur sortent de leurs tentes. La famille mange près du feu. Ils adorent camper ensemble.

Molly a **vingt-deux ans**. Elle vient d'obtenir sa Licence à l'université où elle a étudié l'ingénierie. Elle n'a pas trouvé de travail dans un bureau, alors elle travaille dans son magasin d'équipement de sport. Elle économise son salaire et parle de son passe-temps préféré toute la journée : le camping.

Chaque samedi, Molly travaille au **deuxième** étage, où il y a toutes les tentes, les sacs à dos et l'équipement de camping. Ce samedi, son **cousin** vient au magasin.

« Salut, Jim! » dit Molly, un sourire heureux sur son visage.

« Molly! J'ai oublié que tu travaillais ici », dit Jim, le **fils** de **trente** ans de la tante de Molly, Jane.

« Comment vont tante Jane et **oncle** Joe ? » demande Molly.

« Ils vont bien. Ce weekend, ils rendent visite à **grand-mère** Gloria, chez elle, dit Jim. Je suis ici pour acheter des articles de plein air pour un voyage. »

« Oh, bien sûr! Je peux t'aider. Qu'y a-t-il sur ta liste? », demande Molly.

Jim montre à Molly une feuille de papier avec une liste de **quinze** articles. Un sac à dos léger, un réchaud portable, **quatre** paires de chaussettes chaudes, des bâtons de randonnée, le savon magique du Dr. Bronner, un couteau de poche et **dix-huit** repas déshydratés.

Ça a l'air d'être un sacré voyage, pense Molly.

« Donne-moi le sac à dos le plus léger que vous avez, dit Jim. Le plus léger de tout, en fait. Mon sac à dos de moins doit faire moins de **vingt-huit** pounds. »

« Pourquoi achète-tu tout cela? » demande Molly, en marchant avec Jim vers un mur rempli de sacs à dos de toutes les couleurs, grands et petits.

« Je vais faire une randonnée, dit Jim. À travers l'Espagne. »

Jim essaie les différents sacs à dos. Il choisit le sac préféré de Molly, un sac à dos rouge avec **sept** poches, quatre au dos et trois à l'intérieur. Le sac est si léger, il pèse à peine **deux kilos et demi**. Il le porte sur ses épaules alors qu'il suit Molly à la section vêtements.

« Ça s'appelle le Chemin de Compostelle », confie Jim à Molly. Son cousin lui parle de la randonnée. C'est un pèlerinage à la cathédrale de Saint-Jacques-de-Compostelle en Galice. On dit que saint Jacques est enterré dans l'église.

Jim fera la randonnée à partir du point de départ ordinaire sur le Chemin Français, à Saint-Jean-Pied-de-Port. De là, il est à environ **cinq cents** miles de Saint-Jacques. Le pèlerinage est populaire depuis le Moyen Age. Des criminels et d'autres personnes l'ont parcouru en échange de bénédictions. De nos jours, la plupart voyagent à pied. Certaines personnes voyagent à vélo. Quelques pèlerins voyagent même sur un cheval ou un âne. Le pèlerinage était religieux, mais maintenant beaucoup le font pour voyager ou faire du sport.

« J'ai besoin de voyager, dit Jim. J'ai besoin de temps pour réfléchir. Marcher 800 km peut être très spirituel. »

Molly aide Jim à trouver une veste imperméable et un pantalon qui peut se dézipper pour devenir un short. Il semble très heureux avec son grand sac d'affaires. Il porte beaucoup plus de choses entre les ses bras que les autres acheteurs. Il fait un vrai voyage.

« Ça fera **trois cent quarante-sept** dollars et **soixante-six** cents », dit Molly.

« Merci, Molly », dit Jim.

Molly commence à réfléchir. Elle vit à la maison avec ses **parents**. Sa mère travaille comme juge au palais de justice local et son père est avocat. Ils sont tous deux rarement à la maison pour dîner. Ils restent travailler au bureau jusqu'à tard. Ses **frères et sa sœur** vivent avec leurs familles à Seattle, à trois heures de route. Elle est seule, sans véritable emploi. Il n'y a personne pour l'arrêter.

Ce sera des vacances parfaites. Et peut-être décidera-t-elle quoi faire du reste de sa vie.

Pourquoi pas ?

Ce jour-là, Mollly décide qu'elle fera le Chemin de Compostelle. A partir de septembre, dans trois mois. Seule.

RÉSUMÉ

Une jeune femme du nom de Molly aime le plein air. Elle et sa famille campent souvent ensemble. Elle travaille dans un magasin de plein air alors qu'elle cherche un emploi après l'université. Son cousin Jim lui rend visite pour se préparer à un voyage. Il va marcher le Chemin de Compostelle et a besoin de matériel. Molly l'aide à acheter un sac à dos, des chaussures et tout ce dont il a besoin. Elle décide de faire la randonnée du Chemin de Compostelle elle-même.

Liste de Vocabulaire

family	famille
two	deux
brother	frère
sister	soeur
one	un
three	trois
mom	maman
dad	papa
eight	huit
nineteen	dix-neuf
twenty	vingt
mother	mère
father	père
twenty-two	vingt-deux
second	deuxième

cousin	cousin
thirty	trente
son	fils
aunt	tante
uncle	oncle
grandma	grand-mère
fifteen	quinze
four	quatre
eighteen	dix-huit
twenty-eight	vingt-huit
seven	sept
two-and-a-half	deux et demi
five hundred	cinq cents
three hundred	trois cents
forty-seven	quarante-sept
sixty-six	soixante-six

parents	parents
siblings	frères et sœurs

QUESTIONS

1) Qu'a étudié Molly à l'université?

    a) cosmétologie

    b) littérature

    c) ingénierie

    d) commerce

2) Combien de frères et sœurs Molly a-t-elle?

    a) un

    b) deux

    c) trois

    d) quatre

3) Quel est le lien entre Jim et Molly?

    a) frère

    b) oncle

    c) grand-père

    d) père

4) Qu'est-ce que le Chemin de Compostelle ?

    a) un pèlerinage

    b) une ville

    c) une église

    d) un jour férié

5) D'où vient Molly?

    a) États-Unis

    b) Angleterre

    c) Australie

d) France

RÉPONSES

1) Qu'a étudié Molly à l'université?

    c) ingénierie

2) Combien de frères et sœurs Molly a-t-elle?

    c) trois

3) Quel est le lien entre Jim et Molly?

    b) oncle

4) Qu'est-ce que le Chemin de Compostelle ?

    a) un pèlerinage

5) D'où vient Molly?

    a) États-Unis

Translation of the Story

The Camino Inspiration

Molly loves adventures.

She is the bravest member of her **family**, even braver than her **two brothers**. She often goes camping with her family in the woods. This weekend, they go to the mountain together. The moon shines and the birds and animals are quiet. Molly sits with her brothers and her **sister** by the fire, talking and playing. They see a bat fly over their heads.

"Ewww!" shouts Molly's sister.

"A bat!" yells **one** of Molly's brothers.

Then, **three** more bats fly over their heads.

"Ahhh! Let's get **mom** and **dad**!" shouts the other brother, John.

"It's only a bat," says Molly.

More bats arrive, until there are **eight** flying overhead. Molly's sister and brothers disappear into their tents, scared out of their wits. Molly does not move. She watches as the bats circled, now **nineteen**, no, **twenty**!

"Hi, Molly," says her **mother**, walking up behind her **father** to the campfire.

"Wow, there sure are a lot of bats around these woods," says her dad. "Aren't you scared?"

Molly shook her head no, and watched the bats fly off into the starry night sky.

"Let's eat dinner!" she said. Her brothers and sister come out of their tents. The family eats by the fire. They love to camp together.

Molly is **twenty-two**. She just graduated from college, where she studied engineering. She has not found a job in an office, so she works at her local outdoor store. She saves her paycheck and gets to talk about her favorite hobby all day: camping.

Every Saturday, Molly works on the **second** floor, with all of the tents, backpacks, and camping supplies. This Saturday, in walks her **cousin**.

"Hi, Jim!" says Molly, a happy smile on her face.

"Molly! I forgot you work here," says Jim, the **thirty**-year-old **son** of Molly's **aunt** Jane.

"How are Aunt Jane and **Uncle** Joe?" asks Molly.

"They're good. This weekend they are visiting **Grandma** Gloria at her house," says Jim. "I'm here to buy some outdoor goods for a trip."

"Oh, sure! I can help you. What is on your list?" Molly asks.

Jim shows Molly a piece of paper with a list of **fifteen** items. A light backpack, a portable stove, **four** pairs of warm socks, hiking poles, Dr. Bronner's magic soap, a pocket knife, and **eighteen** dehydrated trail meals.

Wow, this sounds like quite a trip, thinks Molly.

"Gimme the lightest backpack you have," says Jim. "The lightest everything, actually. I have to keep my pack under **twenty-eight** pounds."

"What are you buying all of this for?" asks Molly, walking with Jim over to a wall filled with backpacks of all colors, large and small.

"I'm going to hike," says Jim. "Across Spain."

Jim tries on the different backpacks. He chooses Molly's favorite, a red backpack with **seven** pockets, four on the back and three inside. The pack is so light, it hardly weighs **two-and-a-half** pounds. He wears it on his shoulders as he follows Molly to the clothing section.

"It's called the Camino de Santiago," Jim tells Molly. Her cousin tells her about the hike. It is a pilgrimage to the Cathedral of Santiago de Compostela in Galicia. People say that Saint James is buried in the church.

Uncle Jim will be walking the hike from the common starting point of the French Way, Saint-Jean-Pied-de-Port. From there, it is about **five hundred** miles to Santiago. The pilgrimage has been popular since the Middle Ages. Criminals and other people walked the way in exchange for blessings. Nowadays, most travel by foot. Some people travel by bicycle. A few pilgrims even travel on a horse or donkey. The pilgrimage was religious, but now many do it for travel or sport.

"I need to travel," says Jim. "I need time to think and reflect. Walking 500 miles can be very spiritual."

Molly helps Jim find a waterproof jacket and a pair of pants that can unzip to be shorts. He seems very happy with his large bag of things. He has much more in his hands than the other shoppers. He is going on a real trip.

"That will be **three hundred forty-seven** dollars and **sixty-six** cents," says Molly.

"Thanks, Molly," says Jim.

Molly begins to think. She lives at home with her **parents**. Her mother works as a judge in the local courthouse and her father is a lawyer. They are both rarely home for dinner. They stay busy at the office until late. Her **siblings** live with their families in Seattle, three hours away. She is alone, with no real job. She has no one to stop her.

It will be the perfect vacation. And maybe she will decide what to do with the rest of her life.

Why not?

That day, Mollly decides that she will do the Camino de Santiago. Starting in September, three months from now. Alone.

CONCLUSION

Y^{ou did it!}

You finished a whole book in a brand-new language. That in and of itself is quite the accomplishment, isn't it?

Congratulate yourself on time well spent and a job well done. Now that you've finished the book, you have familiarized yourself with over 500 new vocabulary words, comprehended the heart of 3 short stories, and listened to loads of dialogue unfold, all without going anywhere!

Charlemagne said "To have another language is to possess a second soul." After immersing yourself in this book, you are broadening your horizons and opening a whole new path for yourself.

Have you thought about how much you know now that you did not know before? You've learned everything from how to greet and how to express your emotions to basics like colors and place words. You can tell time and ask question. All without opening a schoolbook. Instead, you've cruised through fun, interesting stories and possibly listened to them as well.

Perhaps before you weren't able to distinguish meaning when you listened to French. If you used the audiobook, we bet you can now pick out meanings and words when you hear someone speaking. Regardless, we are sure you have taken an important step to being more fluent. You are well on your way!

Best of all, you have made the essential step of distinguishing in your mind the idea that most often hinders people studying a new language. By approaching French through our short stories and dialogs, instead of formal lessons with just grammar and vocabulary, you are no longer in the 'learning' mindset. Your approach is much more similar to an osmosis, focused on speaking and using the language, which is the end goal, after all!

So, what's next?

This is just the first of five books, all packed full of short stories and dialogs, covering essential, everyday French that will ensure you master the basics. You can find the rest of the books in the series, as well as a whole host of other resources, at LearnLikeNatives.com. Simply add the book to your library to take the next step in your language learning journey. If you are ever in need of new ideas or direction, refer to our 'Speak Like a Native' eBook, available to you for free at LearnLikeNatives.com, which clearly outlines practical steps you can take to continue learning any language you choose.

We also encourage you to get out into the real world and practice your French. You have a leg up on most beginners, after all—instead of pure textbook learning, you have been absorbing the sound and soul of the language. Do not underestimate the foundation you have built reviewing the chapters of this book. Remember, no one feels 100% confident when they speak with a native speaker in another language.

One of the coolest things about being human is connecting with others. Communicating with someone in their own language is a wonderful gift. Knowing the language turns you into a local and opens up your world. You will see the reward of learning languages for many years to come, so keep that practice up!. Don't let your fears stop you from taking the chance to use your French. Just give it a try, and remember that you will make mistakes. However, these mistakes will teach you so much, so view every single one as a small victory! Learning is growth.

Don't let the quest for learning end here! There is so much you can do to continue the learning process in an organic way, like you did with this book. Add another book from Learn Like a Native to your library. Listen to French talk radio. Watch some of the great French films. Put on the latest CD from Edith Piaf. Take cooking lessons in French. Whatever you do, don't stop because every little step you take counts towards learning a new language, culture, and way of communicating.

LEARN LIKE
A NATIVE
www.LearnLikeNatives.com

Learn Like a Native is a revolutionary **language education brand** that is taking the linguistic world by storm. Forget boring grammar books that never get you anywhere, Learn Like a Native teaches you languages in a fast and fun way that actually works!

As an international, multichannel, language learning platform, we provide **books, audio guides and eBooks** so that you can acquire the knowledge you need, swiftly and easily.

Our **subject-based learning**, structured around real-world scenarios, builds your conversational muscle and ensures you learn the content most relevant to your requirements.
Discover our tools at *LearnLikeNatives.com*.

When it comes to learning languages, we've got you covered!

CPSIA information can be obtained
at www.ICGtesting.com
Printed in the USA
BVHW091156021220
594679BV00006B/352